Crystal and Fox

Brian Friel

CRYSTAL AND FOX
A Play in Six Episodes

FABER AND FABER
London

First published in 1970
by Faber and Faber Limited
24 Russell Square London WC1
Printed in Great Britain by
Latimer Trend & Co Ltd Plymouth
All rights reserved

SBN 571 09387 6

© Brian Friel 1970

TO
SEAN McMAHON

First performed at the Gaiety Theatre, Dublin, on Tuesday, 12th November 1968, with the following cast:

Cyril Cusack
Maureen Toal
John McDarby
Cecil Sheridan
Chris O'Neill
Robert Carrickford
Yvonne Cooper
Niall O'Briain
Brendan Sullivan
Tom Irvine

Hilton Edwards directed

Characters

Fox Melarkey
Crystal Melarkey, his wife
Papa, her father
Pedro
El Cid
Tanya, Cid's wife
Gabriel, Fox's son
An Irish Policeman
Two English Detectives

$\star$ $\star$ $\star$

Fox Melarkey is the proprietor of the travelling show that carries his name. He is about fifty, a small man, narrow shouldered, lightly built, with a lean sallow face grooved by a few deep wrinkles, a face that has been stamped with age since early manhood.

Crystal, his wife, is a few years younger. She is taller than the Fox and heavier. She has a well-structured peasant face, and on those rare occasions when she is groomed she has a fresh and honest attractiveness.

Papa, Crystal's father, is in his late seventies. His voice is husky with age. He is almost totally deaf and shuffles around with his head down, doing his allotted chores with an almost desperate concentration. He is determined to be worthy of his keep.

El Cid and Tanya, a husband-and-wife team, are in their thirties.

Their talent is limited, their self-confidence and optimism limit-less.

PEDRO is sixty. A gentle and guileless man, untouched by the elations and depressions of his profession.

★   ★   ★

There is an interval after Episode 2.

Act One

EPISODE ONE

THE SET: *The acting area is divided into two portions. The portion left (from the point of view of the audience) occupies about one-third of the area; the portion right two-thirds. The dividing line is a flimsy and transparent framework which runs at an angle upstage. The portion left of this division is the stage inside Fox's marquee; the portion right is the backstage; the dividing framework is the back wall of the stage.*

AT RISE: *We join the Fox Melarkey Show during a brief interval before the final episode of their drama, 'The Doctor's Story'.*

CRYSTAL—Mother Superior—is on her knees on the stage, her elbows resting on a chair. She is wearing a nun's white tropical habit that could do with a wash.

EL CID—Dr. Giroux—is backstage. He is wearing a short white medical coat. He is helping TANYA—Sister Petita Sancta—out of a nun's habit and into a gaudy floral dress.

PAPA, their stage manager, is pumping a primus stove.

FOX is bustling around, trying to get his cast organized. He is on edge because from offstage left can be heard the slow clapping of an unseen audience and the chanting of'We want Fox! We want Fox!' The audience is restless and not very respectful; they have long since grown tired of suspending their disbelief. In a circle around the primus stove are some upturned boxes and some props. Fox's piano accordion is in the wings.

> FOX Come on! Come on! They're getting tired. What the hell's up now? Cid? Tanya?
>
> TANYA Just a minute, Fox.

FOX Jaysus, will you hurry!

CID Keep your hair on.

CRYSTAL A good house, my sweet. A few weeks of this and we'll be able to trade in the truck.

FOX [*automatically*] Beautiful, my love.

[*He kisses her on the forehead.*]

Very moving. Gets me here . . .

[*Heart.*]

. . . every time.

CRYSTAL My Fox.

FOX [*to* ALL] They're a noisy pack of bailiffs so belt it out a bit more. Plenty of guts.

PAPA [*to* FOX] What's my name?

FOX [*to* CRYSTAL] What's Papa's name?

CRYSTAL [*to* FOX] Sean O'Sullivan.

FOX [*to* PAPA] Sean O'Sullivan.

PAPA Sean O'Sullivan.

CRYSTAL [*to* FOX] From outside Dublin.

FOX [*to* PAPA] From outside Dublin.

PAPA [*to* FOX] What am I doing here?

FOX Who the hell's going to ask you that! You—you— you're training for the Olympics!

[PEDRO'S *head appears.*]

PEDRO What's the hold-up, Fox?

FOX Our little missionary here.

(TANYA)

Ready yet?

TANYA One more second, Fox——

FOX As far as I'm concerned you can take a week at it; but there happen to be people out there——

CID The lady asked for one second.

FOX The who?

CID Look, Melarkey, if you don't watch that tongue of yours——

12

CRYSTAL Fox, go out and quieten them. Tell them a story.
[FOX *surveys his* COMPANY *with distaste.*]

FOX If they're restless, tell them a story! Christ!
[*Then switching on his professional smile, he swings out on to the stage and acknowledges his boisterous reception.*]
Thank you, thank you, thank you very much, ladies and gentlemen. You have been a wonderful audience and it's great pleasure for the Fox Melarkey Show to be back again in Ballybeg——

VOICE Who's pleasure?

FOX Who let my mother-in-law in here?
[*Laughter.*]
But it's wonderful to see you all again, and you've been very appreciative of our little show; and tomorrow night at the same time——

VOICE What about the raffle?

FOX Look at what's shouting about the raffle! Scrounged a penny from the child behind him so that he could go halves in his wife's twopenny ticket!
[*Laughter.*]
Keep calm, spendthrift: the raffle's coming immediately after this last episode of our little drama.

VOICE Is it faked?

FOX 'Course it's faked!
[*Laughter.*]
And the word's fixed. Can't even speak English, that fella. Must be one of those Gaelic speakers from the back of the hills. I didn't tell you, did I, about his brother, Seamus, the one that never heard a word of English until he left school? Got a job in a drapery shop in Killarney. And the boss said to him, 'Let's hear how you'd talk to the

13

customers.' 'Musha, Sir, me English, Sir, sure it
do be weak. Me jacket, Sir? Am I right? And me
breeches—and me shirt? Ah sure don't worry,
Sir; I do have all the right words up here
[*Indicating his head*]
—in me ass.'
[*Laughter.*]
And now, ladies and gentlemen, the final episode
in our little drama, *The Doctor's Story*.
[*He bows briefly, retreats behind the curtain and has a
quick look around.*]
Bloody cowboys! Ready?

CRYSTAL Ready.

FOX Tanya?

TANYA Go ahead.

FOX Belt it out. And plenty of tears. All the hoors
want is a happy ending. Okay, Papa; take it up.
[PAPA *hoists up the curtain.* FOX *stands in the wings.*
CRYSTAL *buries her face in her hands and prays.* TANYA
enters the set and knocks on the framework.]

TANYA Mother.
[CRYSTAL *is lost in prayer.*]
Mother Superior.

CRYSTAL Did someone call me?

TANYA It's me, Mother. Sister Petita Sancta.
[CRYSTAL *does not turn round.*]

CRYSTAL Ah, Petita, Petita, come in, my child.

TANYA I'll come back later, Mother.

CRYSTAL No, no, no. Come on in. I was just talking to God
about all our little problems in our mission hospital
here at Lakula in Eastern Zambia.
[*She blesses herself and rises.*]
[*She now faces her* VISITOR.]

CRYSTAL But is it——? Yes, it is my Petita! Heavens bless

14

me, I didn't recognize you in those clothes. O, my
child, you look so fresh and sweet.

TANYA The wife of the vice-consul presented it . . .
[*Dress*]
. . . to me gratuitously.

CRYSTAL Dear Petita. We're going to miss you so much here.
But then our loss is Doctor Alan Giroux's gain.

TANYA He is bidding——
[*She breaks off because the kettle on the stove has boiled
and is whistling shrilly.*
FOX *hisses at* PAPA—*who does not hear him. So* FOX
dashes to the kettle and lifts it off.]

CRYSTAL Indeed our loss is Doctor Alan Giroux's gain.

TANYA He is bidding farewell to the other sisters. Just
reflect, Mother: this time tomorrow, he and I shall
be in Paris! Ah, here he comes!
[EL CID *enters. He is a professional magician: acting is
not his most fluent talent.*]

CID I am here to say adieu, mon mere superior.

CRYSTAL Dear, dear Doctor Giroux.

CID I have just had a quick run round the children's,
casualty, fever and maternity wards. All is ship-shape
and Bristol fashion for my replacement, Doctor
Karl Krauger, when he arrives at noon tomorrow.
And just to forestall any emergency I gave every
patient a double injection of streptomycin.

CRYSTAL May God reward you, my son.

CID You know I do not believe in your God, Mother.

CRYSTAL Some day you will, Doctor. I have my sisters praying
for you.
[CID *laughs a skeptic's laugh.*]

TANYA I shall pray too.

CRYSTAL And now would you mind if an old woman gave
you both her blessing?

[TANYA *looks appealingly to* CID.]

TANYA For my sake, Alan.

CID If it makes you happy, mon amour.
[*They kneel at* CRYSTAL'S *feet.*
In the wings FOX *has lifted his accordion and plays*
throbbing churchy chords as CRYSTAL *prays.*]

CRYSTAL May God reward you both for your years of
dedication to our little mission hospital here in
Lakula in Eastern Zambia. May you both find the
joy and happiness and content you deserve so richly.
And if ever you feel like coming back to us, singly
or doubly, our arms will be open wide to hold you
to my bosom. My children.

TANYA Thank you, Mother.
[CID *and* TANYA *rise. A long uneasy pause.*]

CRYSTAL Listen—the river-boat.
[PAPA *has missed his cue.* FOX *dashes over to one of the*
upturned boxes, grabs a whistle and pumps a whooping
sound from it.]
Yes, I knew I heard the river-boat.
[*Arms out.*]
Au revoir, mon enfants.
[*She embraces them both.*
CID *manfully brushes back a tear.*]

CID Someday, Mother, I'll . . . I'll . . .
[*He cannot trust himself to speak. He grabs* TANYA *by*
the hand and together they run off.]

CRYSTAL Goodbye . . . goodbye . . .
[*She sinks to her knees, joins her hands and lifts her face*
up to heaven. It is a face of suffering and acceptance.
PAPA *lowers the curtain. There is sporadic clapping.*
FOX *moves around briskly, dispensing tired compliments*
while the ARTISTS *change costume for their final*
appearance.]

FOX Very nice . . . beautiful work . . . very moving . . . lovely show.

TANYA The line is 'O my child, you look so young and so beautiful' but you're too damn bitchy to say that!

CRYSTAL Sorry, love; I meant to say that—I really did—and

_____

CID That damned old Fool——
[PAPA]
——he makes that kettle whistle on purpose just to throw me!

FOX Okay, okay, let's get changed, good work all round, very convincing, very pathetic, where's Pedro?
[PEDRO *enters. In his arms he carries Gringo, his performing dog. She is dressed in a green skirt and green matching hat.*]

PEDRO Here, boss.

FOX [*to* CRYSTAL, *with casual intimacy*] Exquisite, my love. [*He kisses her.*]

CRYSTAL My pet?

FOX My sweet.
[*Aloud*]
Everybody ready?

CID Just a minute, Fox—don't forget our agreement.

FOX Nice performance, Cid.

CID Me and Tanya take the last call. Agreed?

FOX Agreed.
[*Aloud*]
All set?

CID It's understood then, Fox? We're agreed on that?

FOX Anything you say.
[*Aloud*]
All standing by? Right. Up she goes, Papa.

CID Remember, Fox! I'm not asking you again!
[PAPA *hoists up the curtain. The others wait in the wings.*

FOX *is wearing his accordion. He is greeted by the same uncertain enthusiasm.*]

FOX Thank you, thank you, thank you. And now once more I'd ask you to show your appreciation of the top-rank artistes who performed on these boards tonight. Ireland's best known and best loved man of mystery and suspense—El Cid and his beautiful assistant, Tanya!

[*He strikes a heralding chord. Thin clapping from the audience. Pause.*]

CID Bastard!

[*Then he catches* TANYA'S *hand and assuming a radiant smile he runs on.*]

FOX Thank you, Tanya; thank you, El Cid. And now that dashing Spaniard and his team of super-human dogs—the ex-star of the Moscow Circus—Pedro!

[*Another chord. Applause.* PEDRO *enters. He takes the dog with him.*]

And lastly and by no means least, the lady whose musical and Thespian arts held us all in thrall tonight—I give you—my charming and devoted wife—the gracious Crystal Melarkey!

[*Another chord. Applause.* CRYSTAL *skips on.*]

And now for our raffle for the five pound note. Would you, my love . . . ?

CRYSTAL My Fox. And thank you, ladies and gentlemen. If you have your tickets ready, we'll get some little boy or girl to draw from this box. Have we a volunteer? Come on, children; don't be shy. What about that little lady down there?

FOX Nobody in Ballybeg needs a fiver!

[*This is greeted by hooting and laughter.*]

CRYSTAL If you're all too shy, perhaps Pedro would be kind enough to draw for us. Pedro?

18

[PEDRO *draws and hands her a ticket.*]
A pink ticket; and the number is eighty-seven—
eight seven. Would the lucky holder of ticket
number eighty-seven please come up for his
prize?
[PAPA *approaches from the audience. He is wearing a
top coat and hat.* FOX *strikes a chord. Applause, led
by* CRYSTAL.]

FOX Give him a big hand, friends.

CRYSTAL What is your name, sir?

PAPA [*by rote*] My name is Sean O'Sullivan and I come
from outside Dublin.

FOX [*to audience*] Is he courting a Ballybeg girl?
[*Laughter.*]

CRYSTAL Can I see your ticket? [*After checking*] And he is
absolutely correct! Mr. Sean O'Sullivan from
outside Dublin is the lucky winner!
[FOX *hands over the money.*]

FOX Don't sicken yourself with ice-pops, sonny.

CRYSTAL Congratulations, sir.
[FOX *strikes up an introduction to their theme song—'A
Hunting We Will Go'—and the* COMPANY *link arms
and do a simple dance routine as they sing.*]

ALL A-hunting we will go
A-hunting we will go
We'll catch a fox and put him in a box
A-hunting we will go
Tantiffy tantiffy tantiffy
A-hunting we will go.

FOX Tomorrow's our last night in Ballybeg. Same
time, same place, children under seven admitted
free. A complete new variety show, another lucky
raffle, and by popular demand a repeat of tonight's
classical drama, *The Doctor's Story*. See you again

19

tomorrow. God bless.

[*They strike up the chorus again. By now* PAPA *has returned and lowers the curtain. The thin clapping dies away quickly.*]

CRYSTAL The tide's turned! I told you, my love, didn't I?

FOX [*flat*] You did indeed.

CID Melarkey!

[FOX *is fully aware of* CID's *rage but completely ignores it. He goes very calmly, almost gently, to* PAPA *to recover the fiver. Then he changes into his ordinary clothes.*]

FOX Thanks, Papa. Nice performance.

CID I'm talking to you, Melarkey!

TANYA Easy, Cid.

CID You promised! You said it was agreed!

TANYA Don't lose control, Cid. Please don't.

CID I gave you every warning! But that's okay! That suits me fine. I mean to say—money and conditions—I can rough it as good as the next. But when a man's professional standing is spit on by a weasel like that . . . !

FOX Atta girl, Gringo. Worth your weight in gold. Eh?

CRYSTAL My Fox . . .

TANYA We'll talk about it after we've changed.

CID There's been enough talk. He promised me—it was agreed—we take the last call. But I know him— watched him since I joined this lousy fit-up—twisted, that's what he is—twisted as a bloody corkscrew! No wonder his own son cleared off to England!

TANYA Please, Cid——

CID And I'll tell you something more about him: he's not going to stop until he's ratted on everybody! I know that character!

TANYA [*to* FOX] He's upset, Fox. His stomach curdles on him. [*to* CRYSTAL] In the morning he'll be——

20

CID In the morning I'll be signed up with Dick Prospect's
    outfit! [*As he leaves*] And I'll tell you another thing
    about him: it won't be long before he's back where
    he began—touting round the fairs with a rickety
    wheel!
    [*He rushes off.* TANYA *knows she must go with him.*]
TANYA I gave him bacon for his tea. It always gripes him . . .
    [*She hesitates uncertainly—then rushes off.*]
CRYSTAL Tanya!
    [*to* OTHERS] He doesn't mean it, does he?
    [*No one speaks. She turns to* FOX. *On occasions like
    this* FOX's *eyes go flat and he hides behind a mask of
    bland simplicity and vagueness.*]
    You're not letting him go, are you?
FOX What's that?
CRYSTAL Cid and Tanya! You're not going to let them walk
    away like that?
PEDRO If it's only the calls, Fox, Gringo and me we don't
    give a damn; we'll come on first.
CRYSTAL Fox!
FOX My love?
CRYSTAL They're really leaving!
FOX Are they?
CRYSTAL Go after them! Speak to them!
FOX What about, my sweet?
CRYSTAL For God's sake we can't afford to lose them! I know
    he's difficult—but he's a good act. And if they go
    that's twenty minutes out of the variety. And we've
    no play, Fox!
FOX No play?
CRYSTAL Without Cid! Without Tanya! What's got into you?
    Last month it was Billy Hercules. And before that
    it was the Fritter Twins. Fox, I'm asking you.
FOX What?

CRYSTAL Just speak to him.

PEDRO Maybe if I had word with Tanya——

CRYSTAL It has to be the Fox.

[*Pleading*] My love——

FOX My sweet.

CRYSTAL Say you're sorry—say anything you like—blame me, I don't care; but we must hold on to him.

FOX No, no; couldn't blame you, my love.

CRYSTAL I'm asking you—for my sake—go after them.

FOX Couldn't do that, my love.

CRYSTAL But they'll leave if you don't.

FOX Will they?

CRYSTAL My Fox! We need them.

FOX That's true.

CRYSTAL Then do something. You don't want them to leave us too, do you?

[FOX *gives her a most pleasant smile.*]

FOX If I knew a simple answer to that, my Crystal, I'd go in for telling fortunes.

BRING DOWN LIGHTS

EPISODE TWO

When the lights go up CRYSTAL *and* PEDRO, *now out of costume, are sitting disconsolately on upturned boxes.* THEY *have been drinking tea.* CRYSTAL *is brooding over the departure of* CID *and* TANYA: PEDRO *is trying to be cheerful.*

PEDRO It was in a pub just outside Galway, in the middle of last summer. Cid was there and me and Billy Hercules and Tanya. And he comes in with this

22

big red face of his and a tart with him and he says, 'The drinks are on Dick Prospect, the biggest travelling show in Ireland!' So we says nothing, and he sits himself beside me and he says, 'How's the Fox these times?' 'Fine,' I says. 'Haven't run into him for years. And Crystal? Give her my love,' he says, and he laughs and gives the tart a dig with his elbow. 'And the lad—what's this his name is?' 'Gabriel,' says I. 'That's it. How's he shaping in the business?' So I never says a word to that: what the bugger didn't know did him no harm. And the next thing, out of the blue: 'Pedro,' says he, 'I'll make you an offer: leave the Fox and come with me and you can name your own price.' And everybody stopped talking. And I just put down the glass and I says to him, 'Twenty years ago the Fox Melarkey gave me a job when no other show in the country would touch me,' I says, 'And the day I leave the Fox will be the day I'm not fit to do my piece.' And d'you know what he done, Crystal? He gave me a shove and he says, 'You're a fool—that's what you are, a fool,' and threw a big bull head back and laughed. God, he's a cheeky bugger, isn't he?

CRYSTAL Mm?

PEDRO Dick Prospect—he's a cheeky bugger.

CRYSTAL That's right, Pedro.

[PAPA *enters. There are four untouched tea-cups on the ground. He points to them.*]

PAPA What's keeping Cid and Tanya?

PEDRO They're gone.

PAPA [*to* CRYSTAL] What's he say?

PEDRO Left.

PAPA Left?

[PEDRO *nods.* PAPA *shrugs his shoulders, lifts one cup and sits sipping.*]

PEDRO Good house tonight, wasn't it?

CRYSTAL That's the point—the same all last week—things were beginning to pick up! I told him that! Another month like this and we could have got a new truck. Now——! Honest to God, Pedro, I can't see what's going to happen.

PEDRO He gets that way now and again. It passes.

CRYSTAL Things start to go well and you begin to make plans; and then he has to go and make trouble. And you know it's coming on him—you can see it—he goes all sort of quiet. And then you could shout at him and he doesn't even hear you.

PEDRO He has his ways—like the rest of us.

CRYSTAL You don't have to defend him to me, Pedro. And you know what I'm talking about. You've seen him.

PEDRO It's only in the past few years.

CRYSTAL Just before Gabriel went away; that's when it began.

PEDRO [*with genuine enthusiasm and pride*] Eight—ten years ago—my God he was on top of his form then! Cracking jokes, striding about, giving orders like a king; and everywhere he went, Gabby perched up there on top of his shoulders! My God, the Fox Melarkey show was a real show then!

CRYSTAL Wasn't it, though?

PEDRO He had the country in the palm of his hand!

CRYSTAL That won't pay the bills now.

PEDRO If he put his mind to it, he could build it up again. He could! Not a showman in the country to touch him!

CRYSTAL For God's sake look around you man. Holes in

24

the roof. Broken seats. And when the truck falls apart what's going to pull the vans?

PEDRO I've got a couple of quid put by, Crystal . . . there's not much in it . . . and there's only me and Gringo to spend it . . . and if it's any use . . .

CRYSTAL Good Pedro.

PEDRO Well, you know it's there and all you have to do is . . .

[*He breaks off because he hears* FOX *approach.* FOX *swings on, singing, full of bounce and good spirits. He has a paper under his arm.*]

FOX There is a happy land far, far away
Where we get bread and jam four times a day
[*Speaks*] D'you believe that, Pedro, eh? Move over in the bed and let an honest man in at his work.

PEDRO You're looking very happy.

FOX Me? Oh, just a simple man's satisfaction at the end of a good day's work. Another step closer to paradise. Is there nothing for the Fox?
[CRYSTAL *ungraciously thrusts a cup in front of him.*]
Thank you, my love. And then, of course, we've lost our young couple, Sir Cid and Dame Tanya, off to a pressing engagement in Stratford. 'This time tomorrow he and I shall be in Paris.' Jaysus, if I had to listen to that again I'd shoot myself.

PAPA [*to* FOX] They're gone.

FOX Gone but not forgotten, Papa.

PAPA That's the way—here today, gone tomorrow.

FOX Very true, Papa. [*Turns to* CRYSTAL] Your father's a real sage, my sweet: nothing ruffles him any more. All clowns becomes sages when they grow old, and when young sages grow old they turn into clowns. I was an infant sage—did you know that, Pedro?

25

PEDRO Have they left—Cid and Tanya?

FOX [*with bitter smile*] In this company you discuss a thing—Jaysus, for half an hour, and then someone asks you what you're talking about. Round and round in circles. Same conversations, same jokes, same yahoo audiences; just like your Gringo, Pedro, eh?—doing the same old tricks again and again, and all you want is a little cube of sugar as a reward. How many tons of sugar have you given to bloody dogs over the past twenty, thirty years? Eh?

PEDRO I couldn't even——

FOX [*still smiling*] And how do you know that one night when there's a sudden moon that lights up the whole countryside brilliantly for a second—it comes out from behind a cloud and for that second everything's black and white—how do you know that on a night like that Gringo wouldn't give you all the sugar cubes in the world for just one little saucer of arsenic? Answer me that, Pedro.

CRYSTAL Leave him alone.

FOX He loves the dog—he really does—and all I want to know is does he love him that much that he'd——

CRYSTAL Leave Pedro alone!

[FOX *makes a florid gesture of obedience to her.*]

FOX My queen.

[*to* PEDRO] Contentment lies in total obedience— St. Paul's epistle to the South Africans.

[*He opens the paper and looks through it.*
Pause.

CRYSTAL *rises and crosses to* PAPA. *She speaks into his ear.*]

CRYSTAL You should go to bed.

PAPA I'm not a baby.

26

CRYSTAL Do you want a hot water-bottle?

PAPA Hate them things.

FOX [*reads for general amusement*] 'The local Grand Opera Society held its annual meeting last Wednesday in Sweeney's Hotel in Drung. It was agreed to do *Faust* next April. There are four members in the Society.'

PEDRO Where's Drung?

FOX County Tyrone; not far from where I first met my Crystal. The month of May.

CRYSTAL June.

FOX No, no, my love; it was the 12th day of a glorious May. And the Fox was cycling out to make his fortune in the world with nothing but his accordion and his rickety wheel and his glib tongue, when what did he spy at the edge of the road but three snow-white horses and three golden vans.

CRYSTAL [*to* PEDRO] The vans were brown.

FOX And there was no-one in the first golden van. And there was no-one in the second golden van. But beside the third and last golden van there was Papa rubbing down a snow-white mare. And beside him a princess. And she had her hair tied up with a royal blue ribbon, and a blue blouse, and a navy skirt——

CRYSTAL [*gruffly with embarrassment*] You're a blatherskite.

FOX —and a broach here with 'Mother' written across it.

CRYSTAL [*with sudden simplicity*] That's true!

FOX And Papa was wearing puttees; and there was a smell of heather; and the mare's name was Alice.

CRYSTAL Alice it was!

FOX [*quietly*] And I got off my bicycle—I had no idea what I was going to say; and Papa went on rubbing

27

the mare. And the princess looked at me.
[*Pause.*]

PEDRO What happened, Fox? By God you weren't stuck
for a word!

FOX [*briskly again*] And the Fox whipped off his cap
and bowed low and said, 'What big eyes you've
got.'

CRYSTAL I fell on my feet that day.

FOX Did you?

CRYSTAL Take your tea, you eejit you!

PEDRO [*to* CRYSTAL] And then you and him and Papa set
up on your own—after you got married?

CRYSTAL We had more courage than sense.

FOX And more hope than courage, my love.

PEDRO By God you were going great guns altogether
when you took me on.

FOX And aren't we still, Pedro? [*Deliberately finishing off
the conversation.*] Listen to this—something I saw
here—about the caves at Knockmore—we could
make it in a day, couldn't we? Here we are: [*reads*]
'Four young American students trapped in under-
ground caves at Knockmore.'

PEDRO By God, those Americans are everywhere these times.

FOX 'So far rescue teams have been unable to get to the
young people who have been cut off since the
entrance to the largest cave became blocked by
falling boulders.'

CRYSTAL Any crowds gathering?

FOX Doesn't say.

CRYSTAL I still think we should head towards Dublin.

PEDRO They don't flock to the tragedies the way they
used to.

CRYSTAL Television has them spoiled. It needs to be something
very big.

28

PEDRO A train crash or an explosion in a school.

FOX Has to be children. Remember the time that orphanage in the Midlands burned down?

PEDRO That sort of thing.

CRYSTAL For three solid weeks not an empty seat.

PEDRO Marvellous.

CRYSTAL And a matinee every other day.

PEDRO But your chance of being actually on the spot— once in a lifetime.

PAPA [*rising*] I'd better put on the parking-lights in the truck.

CRYSTAL I'll see to it, Papa.

PAPA What's that?

CRYSTAL I'll do it.

PAPA Don't forget. I'm away to bed, then. Goodnight all.

CRYSTAL Sleep well, Papa.

PEDRO 'Night, Papa.

FOX Goodnight, Papa. [*Suddenly*] Oh, Papa, Papa!
[PAPA *stops.* FOX *fumbles in his pocket.*]
The day before yesterday—remember when I was going into the town?—you gave me a shilling to put on a horse for you.

PAPA Did I?

FOX Planter's Delight in the 3.30. It romped home at nine-to-one. Here's your winnings.
[PAPA's *face lights up with joy.*]

PAPA I forgot all about it . . . isn't that a good one, eh? . . . went clean out of my head . . . 10s. eh? . . . good man, Fox.

PEDRO Maybe you're set for a lucky streak, Papa.

PAPA Clean out of my head . . . bloody good man, Fox.

FOX You can still pick them, Papa!

PAPA Bloody good . . .

[*He leaves.*]

PEDRO That's the first win he's had in months. There'll
be no stopping him now.

CRYSTAL You weren't in the town the day before yesterday.

FOX Papa got his winnings, didn't he? He's happy,
isn't he? [*Changing the subject*] Here—look at that.
[*He stares at* PEDRO's *hands.*]

PEDRO What are you staring at?

FOX Just a thought.

PEDRO What does that mean? What sort of a thought?

FOX Look at those hands, my pet.

CRYSTAL Whose hands?

FOX Pedro's.
[PEDRO *puts his hands behind his back like a child.*]
No—no—hold them out—let's look at them.
[PEDRO *brings them out reluctantly.*]

PEDRO What's wrong with them?

FOX That's it—turn them over—look at them.

CRYSTAL What, Fox?

FOX The long slender fingers—the strength of them.

PEDRO They're clean, aren't they?

FOX Never noticed it before.

PEDRO Now you're making them shake!

FOX There's your man. The problem's solved.

PEDRO Who?—what?—what are you talking about?

FOX The hands of a surgeon. There's your Doctor Alan
Giroux.

CRYSTAL Our Pedro?

FOX A natural.

PEDRO A natural what?—what problem?

CRYSTAL I don't know, Fox; he's——

FOX I do. I'm sure of it. Absolutely perfect.

CRYSTAL Would you, Pedro?

PEDRO Would I what?

30

FOX 'Course he would.

CRYSTAL Cid's part in the play—the young French doctor.

PEDRO Me?

CRYSTAL [to FOX] Maybe he's——

PEDRO Me? Me in the play? Christ, you're not serious!
Me? Sure I can't even introduce my own act! Come
on, Fox, cut it out—none of that sort of talk!
Crystal, you know, Crystal, Christ Almighty, I
couldn't! For God's sake have a heart, man! Don't
ask it of me!

CRYSTAL He doesn't want to, Fox. Anyway we'd still have
no Petita.

PEDRO I'd do anything to pull you out of a hole, Fox—
anything—you know that—but, Christ, acting a
part! Dogs is all I can handle—I'm nothing without
a dog—you know that, Crystal.

FOX Okay. Shut up. Stop bleating.

PEDRO If it was anything else, Fox——

FOX Forget it.

PEDRO You know, Crystal——

FOX Forget it! Stop whining about it! Papa'll play it!
[FOX's outburst creates an embarrassed silence. He goes
back to his paper.
PEDRO looks appealingly to CRYSTAL but she is not
looking at him. Pause.]

CRYSTAL It's time we all went to bed.
[She begins to gather up the tea things.
No one has yet noticed the entrance of a motor-cycle
POLICEMAN in helmet, goggles, gauntlets, riding-
breeches, leather knee-boots. He stands motionless,
slowly surveying every detail. His silent presence
generates an immense threat. When he speaks his voice
is soft and controlled.
FOX glances over his paper and sees him first.

*Immediately he switches on his best manner but his
garrulousness betrays his unease.*]

FOX Goodnight, Sergeant! Visitors, my love! You're
a bit late for the show, Sergeant, but you're just
in time for a cup of tea. Tea for the gentleman,
my love.
[*The* POLICEMAN *moves silently around.*]
Wait a minute—didn't I see you at the show
tonight?—in civvies—standing down at the back?
Amn't I right, boss? It was the goggles there that
threw me for a——

POLICEMAN Fox Melarkey?

FOX At your service, Sergeant. Have a pew. Take the
weight off your legs.
[*Silence. The* POLICEMAN *stands before* PEDRO.]

POLICEMAN Who are you?
[*Before* PEDRO *can reply:*]

FOX That's Pedro, boss. A wizard with dogs. One of
the top artists in the profession. Been with the
Fox Melarkey show for the best part of——

POLICEMAN Can you speak? What's your name?

PEDRO Paddy Donnellan. Pedro's the name I use for the
show.

FOX And this is the better half—Crystal—Mrs. Fox
Melarkey—or the vixen as I sometimes call her!
[*The* POLICEMAN *ignores him.*]

POLICEMAN Who else is there?

FOX You mean who else is there in the company, boss?
Well, there's Papa, that's Crystal's father—he's
just gone to bed—the old ticker's liable to jack up
on him without warning—as a matter of fact you
just missed him by a few seconds—great character—
was a clown all his days—toured with some of the
biggest outfits in Europe. And there's . . . and

32

there's . . . damnit, that's it! An hour ago we had another pair, man and wife team; but they upped and offed on me without as much as by your leave. You've no idea, boss, what it's like trying to cater to top quality artistes these days with competition from TV and——

POLICEMAN Only four? No one else?

FOX That's it, Sergeant. Just four—for the time being. We'll just have to say our prayers and tour the agents again. No want of talent round the country, boss, as a gentleman in your position knows well; but when your audiences are made up of decent country people and their little kiddies, you just can't sign up every cheapjack that wants to join you.

POLICEMAN No one else in the vans?

CRYSTAL If you don't take his word why don't you search them?

FOX No one else, Sergeant. Not a soul. Just the four of us: Crystal, Pedro, Papa and yours truly. As Shakespeare says 'We are a few and a happy few and a band of brothers'——

POLICEMAN When are you moving out?

FOX When are we moving out? Isn't that a coincidence—the very thing we were talking about when you arrived! Right, my pet? I'll tell you our problem, boss. We could do another week, ten days here easy. Jaysus, if we turned away five the night we must have turned away—what would you say, my love?—fifty? sixty? On the other hand, if we don't keep to our schedule, our advance agents start screaming at us——

POLICEMAN When?

FOX When? As a matter of fact, Sergeant, it was . . . it was the concensus of opinion that . . . that we honour

our previous commitments and . . . and pull out
tomorrow morning.

POLICEMAN Make it early in the morning so that you'll be
outside my territory by noon.

CRYSTAL Why should we?

FOX Sure, boss, sure. Anything you say, Sergeant.
Suits us fine. As a matter of fact we've got to be
in Ardbeg by tomorrow afternoon. The new hall
there's at our disposal any time we want it. That's
what we were just saying—can we make it in
time. But we'll make it, boss; don't you worry;
that's where we'll be. The Fox Melarkey never
let his public down yet. Leave it to me, Sergeant.
I'll handle it.

[*The* POLICEMAN *pauses before he leaves and looks
at* CRYSTAL.]

POLICEMAN I'm just giving you good advice, missus. Pay heed
to it.

FOX And we're grateful for it, boss, very grateful. And
now that you're here you're the very man that
can advise me on the best route. Should we go
up through the gap or should we go round by the
foot of Glenmore? It's so long since I did that trip
that I've forgotten which is the quickest road . . .

[*His voice fades away as he goes off behind the*
POLICEMAN.]

CRYSTAL Gestapo!

PEDRO He's after something, whatever it is.

CRYSTAL The Fox is far too sweet to them fellas. I'd give
them their answer.

PEDRO No point in crossing them.

CRYSTAL Out of his territory! You'd think he owned the
place! You'd think we were criminals!

PEDRO He's doing his job.

CRYSTAL It's a dirty job, then. And I never could stomach them.

PEDRO So we're moving out tomorrow?

CRYSTAL Gestapo.

PEDRO I say—looks as if we're moving out in the morning.

CRYSTAL Why should we?

PEDRO It was Fox—he said it—he said we were going to——

CRYSTAL 'He said—he said.' If he had his way we'd keep moving all the time and never light anywhere. Near time he made up his mind to run the show right or pack it in altogether.

[CRYSTAL's *uncustomary sharpness embarrasses* PEDRO.]

PEDRO Well I thought . . . maybe he only meant . . . Supper time for Gringo.

CRYSTAL I'd give them their answer.

PEDRO 'Night, Crystal.

[*She does not hear him. She gathers up the tea things, making a lot of noise in her agitation.*

GABRIEL *appears right and stands watching them. He is in his early twenties. He has inherited a portion of* CRYSTAL's *forthrightness and a portion of* FOX's *depth and they make an uneasy marriage in him. He gives a first impression of being weak—an impression that is not altogether accurate. He is wearing an anorak and an open-necked shirt. He carries a sailor's duffle-bag over his shoulder.*]

GABRIEL [*quietly, without intonation*] Any chance of a bed for the night?

PEDRO Crystal! Look! It's Gabriel!

[CRYSTAL *turns round and stares incredulously.*]

CRYSTAL Gabriel? . . . O my God—Gabriel! It's Gabriel— O my God!

[*She runs to him and flings her arms round him.*]

GABRIEL Crystal!

CRYSTAL Son!

GABRIEL Great to see you.

CRYSTAL I heard Pedro—and I looked up—and whatever
way the light was——!

GABRIEL I wanted to surprise you.

CRYSTAL And the size of him? Look at him, Pedro! A man
big!

GABRIEL Pedro! [PEDRO *and* GABRIEL *embrace.*]

PEDRO Welcome . . . Welcome back.

GABRIEL It's great to be back! How are you all? Where's
Papa? Where's Fox? Where is everybody?

CRYSTAL Fox is about, and Papa's just gone to bed, and
here's Pedro, and here's me! He's got so . . . so
mannish looking! When did you come? How did
you find us?

GABRIEL Crossed from Glasgow last night and hitched the
rest of the way. Pedro! How's all the dogs, man?

PEDRO Only one now—Gringo——

GABRIEL One? Only one?

PEDRO —but she—she's—I'll show her to you—hold
on——

CRYSTAL Not now. In the morning.

PEDRO Never had a dog like her. She's . . . she's like a wife.

CRYSTAL Papa'll be so excited. I'll tell him. No, I won't—
he wouldn't sleep after.

GABRIEL How's he keeping?

CRYSTAL Not bad. Seventy-eight last month.

GABRIEL [*diffidently*] And the Fox?

CRYSTAL Great. As ever. The same Fox. Fighting the world.

PEDRO My God, wait till he sees you!

GABRIEL Maybe I should . . . maybe you should tell him
I'm here first in case——

CRYSTAL That was five years ago. It's all forgotten. He talks about you all the time—doesn't he?

PEDRO Every day, twice a day.

GABRIEL He threw me out, remember.

CRYSTAL I'm telling you—he'll be delighted. Are you hungry? When did you last eat?

[FOX *enters briskly. He doesn't see* GABRIEL.]

FOX Trust you to put the big feet in it! The truck sitting there not taxed and no parking-lights and you have to give lip to the peeler! Only that I kept talking bloody quick——

[*Now he sees* GABRIEL.]

—it's not . . . ?

GABRIEL The prodigal son, Fox.

FOX Jaysus!

CRYSTAL I told him you'd be——

FOX Gabriel!

[FOX *moves first towards him.*
They meet and embrace. FOX *holds his son very*
tightly. He is on the point of tears.]

GABRIEL Easy, Fox, easy.

CRYSTAL Isn't he looking great?

FOX He's looking . . . divine. A lad went away— remember, Pedro?—and look, my sweet, a man, a man. And the presence—the style! When did he come?

CRYSTAL Just now.

FOX How did he find us?

GABRIEL [*deadpan*] Well, when I got off the ship this morning I bought an Irish paper and I looked to see were there any big catastrophes that would gather a crowd of sightseers; and I read that in County——

FOX The hoor! Still at his bloody monkey-tricks!

37

[*To* PEDRO]
You always said he'd make a great clown.
[*Softly*]
Jaysus, but it's good to see you, son. After you
went away, somehow we . . . we . . . But now
you're back to us and suddenly life's . . . [*He
breaks off; continues briskly*] How d'you think she's
looking?

GABRIEL No change.

FOX No change at all. She is my constant enchantment.
[*He kisses her.*]

CRYSTAL My Fox.

FOX And without her I am nothing. And Pedro?

GABRIEL Not a day older.

PEDRO Haa!

FOX We survive.

CRYSTAL And your father?

GABRIEL The very same.

FOX No, no.

GABRIEL Maybe a bit heavier.

FOX And more perverse and more restless and more . . .
You're the one that's put on weight.

GABRIEL Too much beer. Where's the rest of the gang?

FOX Crystal—Pedro—your humble servant—and Papa,
of course; you haven't seen Papa yet? He'll be
glad to see you. Well, that's about it. Things have
changed since . . . since you left. Nowadays if
you're not compact, streamlined, overheads cut to
a minimum, you're out of business. Quick, slick,
first-rate. TV finished the shoddy show. But we've
been lucky; my sweet?

CRYSTAL Very lucky.

FOX Things have changed alright; audiences, artists.
Strange. You'd be surprised. And a man changes,

38

too. You'd be surprised. The years do strange
things to a man. But I have my Crystal.

CRYSTAL And Pedro.

PEDRO I'll show you the dog later, Gabriel. She wears a
green hat and a green skirt.

GABRIEL Can she count?

PEDRO And read. She's uncanny.

CRYSTAL She lies in the bed with him and eats at the table
with him!

FOX You're home to stay, aren't you?
[*Pause.*]

CRYSTAL Even for a while.

GABRIEL For a while—sure—why not.

PEDRO We'll have a celebration! I've a bottle of whiskey
since Christmas that I haven't opened.

CRYSTAL What about something to eat?

PEDRO We'll drink first—then we'll eat.
[*To* CRYSTAL]
Have you any glasses?

CRYSTAL I'll get some.

PEDRO Come over to my van. Gringo'll want to be in on
the fun.
[*As he leaves*] It's like old times again.
[PEDRO *goes off.*]

CRYSTAL He's as excited as if you were his own child.

GABRIEL Great guy.

CRYSTAL We're all excited.

GABRIEL I remember that smell: wet fields and paraffin and
turf.

CRYSTAL I knew the tide was turned—I said that—didn't I?

FOX My love—glasses.

CRYSTAL But we're round the corner now. I know we are.
[*She goes off.*
Now that FOX *and* GABRIEL *are alone there is a*

39

diffidence between them: they are both conscious of it.]

GABRIEL Same old stove.

FOX It goes for no one but Papa.

GABRIEL [*avoiding conversation*] And that patch—[*on the roof*]
—I remember helping Pedro to sew it. Must have
been only nine or ten at the time. He was up on
top of a stepladder and I was trying to hold it
steady and it kept sinking into the ground and I
was sure he was going to fall on top of me . . . but
he didn't. . . . How's business?

FOX Good. Fair.

GABRIEL Have things got rough?

FOX No rougher than usual.

GABRIEL But you're managing?

FOX We've always managed. Sometimes you get sick
managing. Smoke?

GABRIEL Thanks.

FOX [*with his brittle smile*] And we're getting on,
Gabby boy; maybe that's it. Not as much spirit
now.

GABRIEL You're still a young man.

FOX [*pleasantly; almost casually*] Weary of all this . . .
this making-do, of conning people that know
they're being conned. Sick of it all. Not sick so
much as desperate; desperate for something that . . .
that has nothing to do with all this. Restless,
Gabby boy, restless. And a man with a restlessness
is a savage bugger.

GABRIEL What do you want?

FOX What do I want? I want . . . I want a dream I
think I've had to come true. I want to live like
a child. I want to die and wake up in heaven
with Crystal. What do I want? Jaysus, man, if I
knew the answer to that, I might be content with

40

what I have. [*Without stopping*] I like your jacket.

GABRIEL I never had any talent for this business. I would have been no help.

FOX That row we had——

GABRIEL Which one? We fought every other day. I was a cocky bastard.

FOX You know the one I mean—the big one. I'm sorry about that . . . my fault. I would have written to you but I didn't know——

GABRIEL Forget it, Fox; for Christ's sake, forget it.

FOX Well now I've said it.

GABRIEL If I had a pound for every fight I've been in since I'd be a rich man . . . a bloody millionaire. Been here long?

FOX Just tonight.

GABRIEL How is it?

FOX Great—great.

GABRIEL You'll stay, then?

FOX Pulling out in the morning, as a matter of fact. Booking lined up in Ardmore. I tried to cancel it— phoned just before the show—but they're holding us to it.

GABRIEL That sounds good. I think I remember Ardmore.

FOX What have you been doing since?

GABRIEL Me? Everything . . . nothing much . . . a bit of a drifter.

FOX Were you at sea?

[GABRIEL *touches the duffle-bag with his foot.*]

GABRIEL For a while. And British Railways for a while. And dish-washing. And street photographer. Anything that came along. We're a restless breed, Fox.

FOX You're not home to stay at all.

GABRIEL Maybe. I don't know. Depends.

41

FOX You're in trouble—isn't that it?

GABRIEL Trouble?

FOX With the police. Isn't that it?

GABRIEL Takes a fox to know a fox. That's why we could
never get on—we're too alike.

FOX What's the trouble?

GABRIEL When I was nabbed first—not long after I went
over there—they sent me to one of those psychiatrist
blokes. And do you know what he said, Fox? He
said I was autistic—'unable to respond emotionally
to people'. Funny word—autistic—isn't it? Got
me off the hook a couple of times.

FOX The trouble.

GABRIEL And this bloke kept asking me about the show and
about you and Crystal and the travelling around.
Dead serious. Make a good straight man.

FOX Why are the police after you?

GABRIEL He got everything all wrong: he worked it out
that you were some sort of a softy and that
Crystal was tough as nails.

FOX What did you do?

GABRIEL Me? I——

CRYSTAL [off stage] Fox! Gabriel!

FOX She's to know nothing.

GABRIEL Do you think I'd tell her?

FOX Tell me.

GABRIEL I was in this digs. In Salford. And it was a Saturday
night—last Saturday three weeks. And I had a bad
day with the horses. And this bitch of a landlady she
kept shouting up for her money. And the bloke
that shared the room with me I owed him money
too. So I gathered my things and drooped them out
the window and then I went out to the yard and
over the wall.

CRYSTAL (*off stage*) Come on, you two!

GABRIEL We're missing the fun.

FOX Go on.

GABRIEL Must have been nearly midnight by then. And about four streets away there was this newspaper shop and the old woman—she knew me—I used to go in there sometimes—she was closing up. And I asked her for a packet of fags and she said, 'Hold on, love, till I put up these shutters.' And when she went out to the front I saw the till was open. And there was no one about. And just as I reached my hand across, in she comes and starts clawing at me and screaming at me. I tried to shake her off and I couldn't. And she kept screaming and scratching at me. And I was terrified. And I caught this weight—I think it was on the scales—and I hit her. But that didn't stop her. So I hit her again. And again . . .

[*Pause.*]

FOX Did you kill her?

GABRIEL That's the point, Fox; I'm not sure.

FOX Jaysus.

CURTAIN

INTERVAL

Act Two

Early evening, a week later.

Backstage of the marquee: only now it is pitched on a different site—the backstage is left.

A rehearsal is in progress. FOX *is kneeling, his elbows on a chair. He is wearing the habit—but not the headdress—that* CRYSTAL *wore at the opening of Episode One. He is also wearing a large leather belt and hopes to look like a monk.*

FOX [*roars*] I'm not staying on my bloody knees all
day! Will you hurry up!
[CRYSTAL *appears at the door carrying a bucket of
water.*]

CRYSTAL [*sharply*] Someone has to carry the water, you
know!

FOX Surely! In the middle of a rehearsal? All right—
all right; get a move on now.

CRYSTAL 'Cos if I don't go for it none of the gentlemen
around here would think of carrying it.

FOX It's your entrance.

CRYSTAL So just cool down.
[*Very sweetly*] Father.
[FOX *is lost in prayer.*]
Father Superior.

FOX Did someone call me?

44

CRYSTAL It's me, Father. Sister Petita Sancta.

[FOX *does not turn round.*]

FOX Ah, Petita, Petita, come in, my child.

CRYSTAL I'll come back later, Father.

FOX No, no, no. Come on in. I was just talking to God about all our little problems in our mission hospital here at Lakula in Eastern Zambia.

[FOX *now rises and faces his visitor.*]

But is it——? Yes, it is my Petita! Heavens bless me, I didn't recognize you in those clothes. O my child, you look so young and so beautiful.

CRYSTAL The wife of the vice-consul presented it to me gratuitously.

FOX Dear Petita. We are going to miss you so much here. But then our loss is Doctor Alan Giroux's gain.

CRYSTAL He is bidding farewell to the other sisters. Just reflect, Father: this time tomorrow he and I shall be in Paris! Ah, here he comes! Come on, Doctor Giroux!

[PEDRO *runs on. He is wearing a short white medical coat. He is absolutely wretched.*]

PEDRO I have just had a quick run round——

FOX 'I am here to say adieu.'

PEDRO I am here to say adieu, mon mere superior.

FOX Dear, dear Doctor Giroux.

PEDRO I have just had a quick run round the children's, casualty, fever and maternity wards. I gave every nun a double injection of streptomycin.

FOX [*wryly*] Why not! They're all drug addicts!

CRYSTAL Let him go on, Fox. I'm late for the hospital as it is.

FOX Okay, okay. May God reward you, my son.

PEDRO You know I do not believe in your God, Fox— Father.

FOX Some day you will, Doctor. I have my priests
      praying for you.
      [*Pause.*]
      Laugh.
PEDRO I can't.
FOX Try.
      [PEDRO *produces a strange sound.*]
      Cut the laugh.
CRYSTAL I shall pray, too.
FOX And now would you mind if an old man gave
      you both his blessing?
CRYSTAL For my sake, Alan.
PEDRO If it makes you happy, mon amour.
      [CRYSTAL *and* PEDRO *kneel.*]
FOX May God reward you both for your years ... and
      so on and so on ... our arms will be open wide
      to hold you to our bosom—chest. My children.
      [GABRIEL *comes on and watches the rehearsal.*]
CRYSTAL Thank you, Father.
FOX Toot-toot. Listen—the river-boat.
PEDRO Someday, Father, I'll——
FOX Goodbye, goodbye.
      [*To* CRYSTAL] If you hurry you'll still make it.
      [*To* PEDRO] Exquisite, Pedro. Very moving.
PEDRO Fox, for the love of God——
FOX A sincerity all his own; hasn't he, my love?
      [FOX *takes off his habit.* CRYSTAL *pulls on a coat.*]
CRYSTAL There's a bus around six. We'll be back on it.
PEDRO I can't do it! And you know I can't do it!
FOX You'll be fine, man. Don't worry.
CRYSTAL Ready, Gabriel? Come on. Visiting time'll be
      over and Papa'll think we've forgotten him.
GABRIEL Tell him I'll see him at the weekend.
CRYSTAL You're not coming?

46

GABRIEL Next Saturday—tell him next Saturday.

CRYSTAL That's what you said last Saturday. You said you were coming today. You promised me, Gabriel.

GABRIEL It's not—it's just . . . I'm not feeling so well.

CRYSTAL And you're the only one he keeps asking for.

GABRIEL Next weekend—tell him that—next weekend for sure.

CRYSTAL When did you get sick?

GABRIEL It's a headache. I often get them.

[CRYSTAL *looks to* FOX *for an explanation.*]

FOX [*quickly*] You're going to miss the bus.

CRYSTAL I don't understand it; that's all. And neither will he.

PEDRO Tell him Gringo sent her love.

FOX Have you the clean pyjamas and the oranges?

[CRYSTAL *nods.*]

And tell him we can't hold a raffle until he comes back.

CRYSTAL He [GABRIEL] could do the raffle.

[FOX *takes a packet of cigarettes from his pocket, shakes them, and throws them to* CRYSTAL.]

FOX Here—give him these.

CRYSTAL I'll be back before seven.

[*She goes off.*]

FOX [*calling*] And tell him to keep his hands off the nurses.

[*To* GABRIEL] The least you could do is go and see him before he dies.

[GABRIEL *ignores him.*]

I'm talking to you!

GABRIEL [*completely calm; almost indifferent*] You know I can't walk about.

FOX She doesn't know that.

GABRIEL It's a wonder you didn't tell her.

47

FOX I didn't tell her—for her sake, not yours.

GABRIEL If there was money in it, you wouldn't have kept so quiet, would you?

FOX I'm not much, sonny, but I'm no informer.

PEDRO Fox, I don't want to keep on about it——

FOX What-what-what?

PEDRO You don't know how miserable I am doing this stuff.

FOX Beautiful, Pedro. Exquisite.

PEDRO I can't even pronounce the words right.

[*Absolutely miserable*] Gabriel, would you . . . ?

GABRIEL Ug-huh.

PEDRO You'd be great—a young man and all.

GABRIEL I won't be around much longer, Pedro.

[PEDRO *shuffles off.*]

PEDRO All I know is if I could see myself up there [*on stage*] I'd never lift my head again.

[FOX *busies himself gathering up the props.* GABRIEL *and he are both conscious of the tension between them.*]

GABRIEL Do you want a hand?

FOX No.

[*Pause.*]

GABRIEL Isn't there a show tonight?

FOX Unlikely.

GABRIEL I thought you went around with handbills this morning?

FOX I did.

GABRIEL Well, if you put out bills——

[FOX *interrupts him sharply and stands poised, listening.*]

FOX Shh!

GABRIEL What is it?

[*Silence.* FOX *relaxes and goes on working.*]

FOX Nothing.

48

GABRIEL Crystal thinks there's a show. That's why she's
rushing back.
[*Pause.*]
I didn't mean what I said—about you and money.

FOX Doesn't matter.

GABRIEL Well what do you expect me to do? Go to the
hospital with her and be picked up there? Is that
what you want? All right, then; I'll go. And I'll
tell her first——

FOX She's not to know.

GABRIEL She's going to know. If the old man dies and I
haven't gone to see him——
[*He breaks off because* CRYSTAL *enters.*]

FOX What's wrong?

CRYSTAL Missed it by a second. It went flying past just
as I got to the road.

FOX Come on. There's enough petrol in the truck to
take us there and back.

CRYSTAL And it not taxed? And all those peelers about the
town?

FOX It's insured. Isn't that enough for them? Come
on—the old man'll be waiting.

GABRIEL Crystal, I've something to tell you.

FOX If nobody else is going I'm going myself.

GABRIEL I can't go anywhere, Crystal, because the police
are after me.

CRYSTAL Police?

FOX It's nothing—nothing at all——

GABRIEL I've been on the run for over a month.

CRYSTAL What did you do?

FOX He stole money from a shop—that's what he
did——

GABRIEL And there was an old——

FOX He lifted a few shillings and bolted.

CRYSTAL Where?

GABRIEL Salford.

CRYSTAL Where's that?

GABRIEL Near Manchester.

CRYSTAL How much?

GABRIEL I don't know—£2—maybe £3—it's not the——

FOX And then he ran and that's the whole story. I told him not to tell you. Can't keep his bloody mouth shut.

GABRIEL I'll clear out in the morning—sign on with a tanker——

[CRYSTAL *is very cool, very calm, very much in command.*]

CRYSTAL Is it the English police that are after you?

GABRIEL I don't know. I think so.

CRYSTAL Were you seen?

GABRIEL I suppose so——

FOX He was.

CRYSTAL Have they got your name?

GABRIEL I don't think so.

CRYSTAL How much money did you lift?

GABRIEL A few pounds——

CRYSTAL How much?

GABRIEL Four-ten.

CRYSTAL When did this happen?

GABRIEL About a month ago.

CRYSTAL Where were you since?

FOX Glasgow.

CRYSTAL And then you came straight here to us?

GABRIEL Yes.

CRYSTAL Did you hang about Dublin?

GABRIEL No. Look, I'll clear out tomorrow——

FOX If we got him the length of Cork or Belfast he could get a boat to——

CRYSTAL He's going nowhere! We've been in trouble
before; and the way to get out of it is to sit
still and say nothing—to nobody! Is that clear?
You can help with the show. You'll get some
money. And as long as we keep on the move
and steer clear of the towns you're as safe as
houses. Out of sight—out of mind—they'll soon
forget about you. Is that clear?
[GABRIEL *shrugs*.
She turns to FOX.]
Is that clear?

FOX What if they come looking for him?

CRYSTAL D'you think they're going to search the country
for the sake of £4 10s.?
[*To* GABRIEL] It's up to you: stick with the show
and keep your mouth shut and that'll be the end
of it. Anyway we could do with the help . . . I
suppose it's near tea-time.

GABRIEL I'm sorry, Crystal.

CRYSTAL Maybe this way you'll have to stay with us.
[*She wearily goes to the other end of the marquee and
throws her coat across a seat. While she is outside
their range:*]

FOX [*viciously*] You're a louse to have told her!

GABRIEL She suspected.

FOX And what are you going to tell her if they come
for you? Eh?

GABRIEL I would have told her the whole truth at the
beginning.

FOX That you may be wanted for murder?

GABRIEL You leave me alone and I'll keep out of your way.
[CRYSTAL *is back*.]

CRYSTAL We need some methylated for the stove. That
was one of Papa's jobs.

FOX He'll wonder nobody turned up.

CRYSTAL There's visiting tomorrow. I'll get the early bus and——

[*She breaks off because* PEDRO *has entered, carrying the lifeless body of* GRINGO *in his arms.* PEDRO *is so stunned that he is beyond emotion.*]

PEDRO It's Gringo.

CRYSTAL Pedro——

GABRIEL Is she sick? She's not——?

CRYSTAL What's wrong, Pedro? What's happened?

PEDRO Gringo.

GABRIEL Christ!

CRYSTAL I saw her this morning after breakfast—she was fine——

GABRIEL She's stiff.

CRYSTAL O God!

[GABRIEL *touches the dog's mouth.*]

What—what's that stuff?

PEDRO My Gringo.

GABRIEL Must have been poisoned.

CRYSTAL How could she have been poisoned, you fool! She never leaves the van!

PEDRO And she's wise, very wise. And humorous, very humorous.

CRYSTAL O God, Pedro, Pedro!

PEDRO She'll be seven next birthday . . . 10th of March. I make a cake and put candles on it.

CRYSTAL Is there nothing——? Brandy——?

GABRIEL Dead a good while.

PEDRO I called her. 'Where are you?' I says. 'I know you're hiding,' I says. 'I've got liver for your supper,' I says. 'And if you don't come out I'll eat it all myself,' I says. 'Cos I know she likes liver.

[CRYSTAL *puts her arm around him. He moves very slowly off. She goes with him.*]
And I put it on the pan. And I thought the smell would coax her. And all the time I kept talking to her the way I always do . . .

CRYSTAL Pedro.

PEDRO And when there was no sign of her I started looking for her. 'I'll give you skelp,' I says. 'That's what you'll get—a right good skelp.' 'Cos she knows I'd never lay a finger on her . . .
[*His voice fades away.*]

GABRIEL Christ, that's awful. . . . She's all he has. . . . And at his age . . .

FOX That's the way.

GABRIEL How the hell could she have picked up poison around here? For Christ's sake, no one sets poison in the middle of a bog!
[FOX *shrugs his shoulders and moves away.* GABRIEL *glances at him, then looks at him, then stares at him.*]
Fox . . .

FOX [*quickly, defensively*] Well?

GABRIEL God, Fox . . . you didn't?

FOX What are you mouthing about?

GABRIEL You did?

FOX Did what?

GABRIEL Christ, man, how could you?

FOX Who are you to talk?

GABRIEL You might as well have killed Pedro himself.

FOX It's a dog, remember—not an old woman.

GABRIEL You did it . . . deliberately . . . to get rid of Pedro.

FOX Shut up.

GABRIEL Just as you got rid of the Fritter Twins and Cid and Tanya and all the others I heard about.

FOX You know nothing about it.

GABRIEL Why, man?

FOX You know nothing about it.

GABRIEL What are you at?

FOX Just leave me. I'm managing fine.

GABRIEL Fine? You call this fine? Wrecking the show? Killing an old man's dog? What are you doing? [*Pause.*]

FOX Once, maybe twice in your life, the fog lifts, and you get a glimpse, an intuition; and suddenly you know that this can't be all there is to it— there has to be something better than this.

GABRIEL You're going mad! What fog?

FOX And afterwards all you're left with is a vague memory of what you thought you saw; and that's what you hold on to—the good thing you think you saw.

GABRIEL You planned it all! That's it. It's all deliberate!

FOX Because there must be something better than this.

GABRIEL It's some sort of a crazy scheme!

FOX [*wearily*] Go away, boy.

GABRIEL You're full of hate—that's what's wrong with you—you hate everybody!

FOX No.

GABRIEL Even Crystal.

FOX What about Crystal?

GABRIEL She'll be the next. You'll ditch her too.

FOX How little you know, boy. My Crystal is the only good part of me.

BRING DOWN LIGHTS

Night.

The Stage is empty and almost totally dark.

Off right there are muffled sounds of excited voices. Then suddenly GABRIEL *enters right and races frantically across stage. He is in his bare feet, undervest and trousers. As he gets to extreme left a uniformed Irish* POLICEMAN *steps out of the shadows—and* GABRIEL *lands in his arms.*

POLICEMAN The running's over. Take it easy, Melarkey.

              [*Two plainclothes English* DETECTIVES *enter right.*]

DETECTIVE I Hold him, Sergeant!

DETECTIVE 2 The bastard bit my hand!

              [*Produces handcuffs.*]

              Hold them out, Paddy. When I get you back,

              I'll fix your teeth.

              [GABRIEL *holds out his hands.* DETECTIVE 2 *hits him in the lower stomach.* GABRIEL *doubles up.*]

POLICEMAN No need for that.

DETECTIVE 2 And that's only the beginning, Paddy. A warming up you might say.

POLICEMAN Better get some clothes for him.

DETECTIVE I I'll get them.

POLICEMAN And shoes.

              [DETECTIVE I *leaves.*]

DETECTIVE 2 I'd take him as he is.

              [*Catches* GABRIEL *by the chin*] Might cool you off, Paddy, eh? And I want you to know me. My name's Coalstream. Been after you for quite a while now, Paddy. And after I've finished with you, you'll be sorry you ever left your gypsy encampment.

POLICEMAN You'll be charged in the station.

DETECTIVE 2 And in the morning we go to Manchester. By

plane. For speed, Paddy. Extradition papers—
reservations—all in order. You're quite a big
piece of dirt; you know that, Paddy?

[*Enter* FOX *and* CRYSTAL, *wearing coats over their
night clothes.* FOX *is carrying a hurricane lamp.*]

FOX What the hell's all the——

CRYSTAL Fox! It's Gabriel!

DETECTIVE 2 You two his parents?

CRYSTAL What's wrong? Who are you?

[*Sees handcuffs.*]

Why is he handcuffed?

DETECTIVE 2 He's under arrest, missus. And tomorrow
afternoon he'll be charged in Manchester with
the attempted manslaughter of an old lady two
months ago.

CRYSTAL Manslaughter? . . . Gabriel?

DETECTIVE 2 He's lucky it's not murder.

CRYSTAL Oh my God . . .

[FOX *holds her arm to steady her.*]

GABRIEL He [FOX] knew. I told him.

CRYSTAL It's lies! It's lies!

DETECTIVE 2 Why don't you ask him [GABRIEL], missus? He
knows all about it.

CRYSTAL Why didn't you tell me, Fox? Why didn't you
tell me?

FOX Easy, my love. Shhhh.

[DETECTIVE I *returns with* GABRIEL'S *shoes and
clothes. Because* GABRIEL *is handcuffed the jacket is
draped over his shoulders. The* POLICEMAN *puts the
shoes on his feet. While this is going on:*]

CRYSTAL Manchester? . . . Why are you taking him there?

DETECTIVE I That's where he coshed the old lady. Twenty-nine
stitches she got. You've a boy to be proud of,
missus—a real gentleman.

56

CRYSTAL I'm going, too. Wherever you're taking him, I'm
        going too.
GABRIEL I'll be all right, Crystal.
DETECTIVE 1 You can't hold his hand in jail for ten years.
DETECTIVE 2 He'll do. I've a special heater in the car for him.
CRYSTAL Fox——!
FOX Easy, easy, easy.
DETECTIVE 2 Bloody gypsies. Same all over.
FOX Where are you taking him to?
POLICEMAN To the station. Then to Dublin . . .
CRYSTAL Stop them, Fox! Stop them!
DETECTIVE 1 He'll get a fair trial, missus.
DETECTIVE 2 He'll get his desserts. Come on.
CRYSTAL Give him back to me!
        [*She breaks away from* FOX *and flings herself at the
        police. There is a brief scuffle. She is thrown to the
        ground.*]
DETECTIVE 2 Stinking gypsies! Let's go.
        [*The two* DETECTIVES *move off with* GABRIEL *between
        them.* CRYSTAL *does not hear the following:*]
POLICEMAN I warned you to get out of my territory,
        Melarkey.
FOX How did you know he was here?
POLICEMAN The old man in hospital spilled the beans.
FOX Papa?!
POLICEMAN The old doting man. Everyone that lights in his
        ward he asks them to tell Gabriel to come and
        see him.
FOX And some rat went and told you?
POLICEMAN He told me himself, Melarkey. And if the boy
        had gone to see him—even once—the old man
        would have been content and we might never
        have known.
        [*He leaves.*]

57

[FOX *turns round, sees* CRYSTAL *sobbing. He sits beside her and puts his arms around her.*]

CRYSTAL Gabriel . . .

    FOX My love.

CRYSTAL My boy.

    FOX It's all right . . . all right . . .

CRYSTAL My Gabriel.

    FOX Easy . . . easy . . .

        [*She sobs convulsively.* FOX *holds her head to his shoulder.*]

BRING DOWN LIGHTS

EPISODE FIVE

When the lights come up dawn is breaking. FOX *and* CRYSTAL *are dressed as we left them.* CRYSTAL *is sitting on an upturned box, staring at the dead stove. They have not been in bed all night and their conversation has an exhausted and ragged inconsequence.*

FOX *has been watching the dawn break. He now moves over beside her.*

    FOX The sun's coming up.

        [*He sits beside her and takes her hand.*]

        My sweet?

CRYSTAL My Fox.

    FOX How do you feel?

CRYSTAL Not bad.

    FOX You should lie down for a while now.

CRYSTAL You know I couldn't sleep.

    FOX [*briskly, the entertainer*] That's what I'll do, then. This very morning. 'Mr. Prospect,' I'll say,

58

'because of considerations of health the Fox
Melarkey show is prepared to—to—to consider
a take-over bid offered by you, provided, of
course, the financial terms are acceptable to
the joint shareholders of the Melarkey board.'
Eh? No—'provided the cash settlement is realistic
in terms of our national reputation and all
currently functioning equipment.' How about
that?

CRYSTAL What's that, Fox?

FOX Is that all right?

CRYSTAL [*listless*] That's good. That's fine.

FOX Everything except the accordion and the rickety
wheel.

CRYSTAL And this [*stove*] too.

FOX What d'you think his offer'll be?

CRYSTAL Couldn't even make a guess, my pet.

FOX Well, I mean to say, there's the truck; and two
vans—one in semi-mint condition; and the
marquee and the stage; and the ornate proscenium
and velour curtains; and—and—and—and of
course the reputation and goodwill—if he offers
me sixty quid for the lot, Jaysus, I'll take the arm
off him.

CRYSTAL It's cold.

FOX You're tired.

CRYSTAL I'll get some solicitor to defend him, won't I?

FOX Flash the money, my love, and you'll get the
Lord Chief Justice.

CRYSTAL I just can't get it out of my head . . . not Gabriel
somehow . . . he was never that kind . . . or maybe
you never know anybody.

FOX They'll be in Dublin by now.

CRYSTAL If he's been a rough boy or anything. But he's

59

so . . . so soft . . . at least I thought he was.

FOX Probably he panicked.

CRYSTAL Those shoes [FOX's] are letting in.

FOX The ground's dry.

CRYSTAL 'There's no worse shod than a shoemaker's wife'
—that was a great expression of Papa's. I never
knew what it meant.

FOX I think we shouldn't tell him about Gabriel.

CRYSTAL Makes no difference now. He's past understanding.

FOX Maybe.

CRYSTAL Sure you know he's completely doting.

FOX I suppose so.
[*He rises*] A strange time of day, this. . . . Every
time I see the sun coming up, I think of the
morning we——
[*He breaks off and looks at her.*]
Do you remember the channel?

CRYSTAL What's that?
[*He begins quietly, diffidently. But as he recalls the
episode—and as she remembers it, too—his warmth
and obvious joy spread to her.*]

FOX A few miles north of Galway—along the coast—
a channel of water—a stream—just where it
entered the sea. We were only two weeks married
at the time.

CRYSTAL [*listlessly*] Galway's nice.

FOX [*he sits beside her*] And you got a mad notion of
going for a swim at dawn. And this morning,
just about this time, you woke me up, and we
slipped out and raced across the wet fields in our
bare feet. And when we got to the sea, we had
to wade across this stream to get to the beach.

CRYSTAL [*suddenly remembering*] The channel!

FOX D'you remember? And you hoisted up your

skirt and you took my hand and we stepped into the——

CRYSTAL Fish! Flat fish!

FOX Hundreds of them! Every step you took! D'you remember?

CRYSTAL Oh my God!

FOX Every time you put a foot down!

CRYSTAL The wriggling of them! Under your bare feet!

FOX And you couldn't go forward! And you couldn't go back!

CRYSTAL And you splitting your sides laughing!

FOX Trying to keep hopping so that you wouldn't touch bottom!

CRYSTAL Squirming and wriggling!

FOX And then you lost your balance—and down you went!

CRYSTAL And pulled you down, too.

FOX And then you started to laugh!

CRYSTAL It was the sight of you spluttering!

FOX The water was freezing!

CRYSTAL We were soaked to the skin!

FOX And we staggered over to the beach.

CRYSTAL And you, you eejit, you began to leap about like a monkey!

FOX The seagulls—remember?—they sat on the rocks, staring at us.

CRYSTAL And you tied a plait of seaweed to my hair.

FOX And we danced on the sand.

CRYSTAL Wet clothes and all.

FOX And then the sun came out.

CRYSTAL The channel. . . . Funny, I'd forgotten that altogether.

FOX Just the two of us.

[*Silence; each with his own thoughts.*]

61

CRYSTAL Fox, I was thinking——

FOX [*eagerly*] What?

CRYSTAL Before you had this idea of selling out, I was thinking where we could raise the money for a solicitor.

FOX [*flatly*] Oh.

CRYSTAL And Pedro was the only person I could think of. He offered me money before, you know.

FOX A good man.

CRYSTAL A great man. I wonder where he's disappeared to?

FOX God knows.

CRYSTAL He used to talk to that dog as if it was a baby.

FOX That's the way.

CRYSTAL Maybe he went to Dublin; he has a cousin there.

FOX She died years ago.

CRYSTAL I didn't know that. How long does it take to fly from Dublin to Manchester?

FOX About an hour.

CRYSTAL I don't think he was ever in an airplane before, was he?

FOX Not that I know of.

[FOX *is conscious that he should match* CRYSTAL'S *sombre mood. But he is unable to suppress the strange excitement he feels. He moves closer to her.*]

My sweet——

CRYSTAL My Fox.

FOX My sweet, when we get rid of this stuff to Prospect——

CRYSTAL Maybe he won't touch it.

FOX Don't you worry: I'll get rid of it. And when I do there'll just be you and me and the old accordion and the old rickety wheel—all we had thirty years ago, remember? You and me. And

62

we'll laugh again at silly things and I'll plait
seaweed into your hair again. And we'll go only
to the fairs we want to go to, and stop only at
the towns we want to stop at, and eat when we
want to eat, and lie down when we feel like it.
And everywhere we go we'll know people and
they'll know us—'Crystal and Fox!' Jaysus, my
love, if I weren't a superstitious man, I'd say—
I'd say——

CRYSTAL What?

FOX I'd say that heaven's just round the corner.

BRING DOWN LIGHTS

EPISODE SIX

Two days later.

*A cross-roads in the open country. A signpost pointing in four
directions. It is a beautiful sunny day.*

From some distance off can be heard the sound of FOX *and* CRYSTAL
*approaching. They make so much noise—chattering, laughing, whoop-
ing, singing—that one would expect to see a dozen happy children
appear.*

Now they arrive at the cross-roads. FOX *is carrying the rickety
wheel, the accordion, and the stove.* CRYSTAL *is carrying two shabby
suitcases.* FOX *has a bottle of wine in his pocket, and when their
hands are free, the bottle passes between them. Neither is drunk, nor
even tipsy, but both are more than a little elated: all their immediate
worries have been solved; and the afternoon is warm; and the wine
is heady.* FOX *is particularly jaunty and vivacious, like a young man
being flamboyant to entertain and impress his girl.*

FOX This is it! Here we are!

CRYSTAL Where?

FOX Here!

CRYSTAL You're pulling my leg!

FOX Anything that's going anywhere has to pass here.
Dublin—Galway—Cork—Derry; you're at the
hub of the country, girl.

CRYSTAL The hub of the country! Fox, you're an eejit!

FOX [sings] 'A-hitching we will go
A-hitching we will go!'
Throw your stuff down there and leave everything
to the Fox. Two single tickets to—where do you
wish to go to, Madam?

CRYSTAL Manchester!

FOX Manchester it'll be!

[CRYSTAL drops down on the side of the road.]

CRYSTAL [giggling] No one's ever going to stop, my Fox.
They're all going to swizzzzz right past. And
we're going to spend the rest of our lives in the
middle of nowhere. God, I'm giddy!

FOX [toasting] To a great day's work. To your lawyer,
Mr King——

CRYSTAL Ring! Frederick Ashley Ring!

FOX —who'll see that our boy is well defended; and
to Dick Prospect who parted with forty crisp notes
for a load of rubbish and for a truck that won't
go into reverse.

CRYSTAL You didn't tell him?!

FOX D'you think I'm mad? He kept saying, 'She runs
sweet enough, Fox, I can see that. Turn her at
this gate and take me back.' 'No, no, Dick, a
fair trial; we'll go right round the circuit. I want
you to know what you're getting.'

CRYSTAL Too damn good for him!

FOX And when we got back to his place who d'you
think I saw?

CRYSTAL Who?

FOX Cid.

CRYSTAL You did not!

FOX Eating a big feed of bacon and eggs—his van
door was open; and she was standing outside,
screaming in at him.

CRYSTAL What about?

FOX 'You've lost control! And don't blame me if
your stomach curdles and gripes on you!'
[CRYSTAL rolls over with laughter.]
This is the life, girl; it should always have been
like this.
[He hears a car approaching.]
Transport! Transport! We're in business! This is
it. We're away! Gather up your things!
[He hides the bottle, straightens his tie, assumes a
pleasant face, does a brief jig for CRYSTAL's
entertainment, and takes up his position at the verge of
the road.]

CRYSTAL God, this is a scream!

FOX [to car] Come on, come on—that's it, me aul
darlin—a lift for the Crystal and the Fox—slow
down—that's it—decent fella—we'll go wherever
you're going—look at the wee narrow
shoulders and the wee sad face smiling in at
you——

CRYSTAL [laughing] You eejit you!

FOX —sure you never saw anything as pathetic in all
your life—the honest Fox Melarkey depending
on charity for his transportation and
edification——

CRYSTAL [laughing] Quit it, Fox!

E   65

FOX Doesn't hear a word I'm saying.
[*To car*] May God reward you for your years
of dedication to our little mission hospital here
in Lakula in Eastern Tipperary—Jaysus, you
couldn't say no to a pair of innocent eyes like
these—Jaysus, you could—Jaysus, you're a hoor!
[*The car has gone past. Peals of laughter from*
CRYSTAL.]
[*To car*] And in the next bad frost I hope they
drop off you!
CRYSTAL He heard you, you clown you!
[FOX *is moved by a strange elation: not so much joy
as a controlled recklessness. The sun, the wine, the
release from responsibility. The desire to play up to
an easy audience like* CRYSTAL—*these are all the
obvious ingredients of his exultation. But he is aware
—and* CRYSTAL *is not—that it has also a cold brittle
quality, and edge of menace. He gives the rickety
wheel a sharp turn, and addresses an imaginary
crowd:*]
FOX Red-yellow-black or blue, whatever it is that
tickles your fancy, now's your chance to turn a
bad penny into a decent pound, there's a wee
lassie out there that looks as if she might, come
on, my love, now's your chance, if you wait till
your mother tells you, the notion'll have gone
off you.
CRYSTAL Take a swig before it's done.
FOX No more for me.
CRYSTAL All the better.
FOX [*irritably*] Are there no bloody cars in the
country?
CRYSTAL Lie back here beside me and relax.
FOX I have to be on the move.

[*Eagerly*] My Crystal, let's get married again!

CRYSTAL You're drunk.

FOX My love, marry me again. Please marry me again.

CRYSTAL Full as a pig!

FOX I'm asking you, my sweet.

CRYSTAL Here?

FOX Now.

CRYSTAL At this moment?

FOX Immediately.

CRYSTAL In these clothes?

FOX Just as you are.

CRYSTAL This is so sudden. But why not? You only die
once?
[*Rises and sings*] 'Here comes the bride, small fat
and wide——'
[*She breaks off suddenly.*]
A car!

FOX [*irritably*] Let it pass.

CRYSTAL A big swanky one! Come on, Fox; do your job!

FOX I hear no car.

CRYSTAL There it is. Quick! Hide that bottle!

FOX [*vaguely*] Will I try it?

CRYSTAL What d'you mean—will you try it? You don't
want to be stuck in this godforsaken place, do
you? Will you try it! What's wrong with you,
man?

FOX [*very sharply*] Okay. Okay. Stop nagging!

CRYSTAL 'Will I try it'!
[*He faces the approaching car and switches on his
professional smile.*]

FOX That's it—take it easy—slow now—slower——

CRYSTAL We're away this time!

FOX Good day to you, ma'am—Fox and Crystal, a
professional couple temporarily inconvenienced

and maladjusted—Melarkey's the name—and
who's to say, perhaps the first lay pope——

CRYSTAL Ha-ha-ha-ha!

FOX That'll be an entry for your diary: 'Today I
gave a lift to the Supreme Pontiff and his missus
outside the village of Slaughmanus——'

CRYSTAL She hears you, you fool you!

FOX Wait—wait—wait—wait——
[*The car has gone.*]

CRYSTAL She heard every word you said!

FOX [*shouts*] With a face like that you'd need a Rolls!
Elephant!

CRYSTAL The sun's roasting.

FOX We've got to move. We must keep moving.

CRYSTAL Honest to God, my sweet, I'm tipsy! Haven't
seen Dickie Prospect for years. How's he
looking?

FOX As usual.

CRYSTAL Was he asking for Crystal?

FOX You're plastered.

CRYSTAL Don't tell me my Fox is jealous!

FOX Of that animal? Jaysus!

CRYSTAL Don't worry, my sweet. It was a long, long, long,
time ago, before I met my Fox.

FOX Animal.

CRYSTAL And he never, never, never crosses my mind.

FOX What the hell sort of a dead-end is this?

CRYSTAL Very pretty. And the sun's warm. And there's a
smell of heather. And I feel ... gorgeous. D'you
think I'm gorgeous, my pet?
[*No response from* FOX.]
My Fox.

FOX Mm?

CRYSTAL Sit down here beside me.

FOX Can't sit.

CRYSTAL We're all rotten, my sweet.

FOX You're drunk.

CRYSTAL I am not drunk, Fox. But I am rotten. Papa's dying in hospital. Gabriel's going to jail. The show's finished. We've no money. And I'm happy as a lark. Amn't I rotten, my Fox?
[*He does not answer.*]
Fox.

FOX Maybe we should try the other road.

CRYSTAL You changed, my pet.

FOX Or go back to the village.

CRYSTAL You think I didn't notice. But I did. Crystal saw it all.

FOX Good for Crystal.

CRYSTAL Just when things were beginning to go well for the show, too. And then you got . . . restless. That's what happened. My Fox got restless. Out go the Fritter Twins. Out goes Billy Hercules. And I was frightened 'cos I thought: He's going to wreck it all, break it all up. That's when it began. Am I right, my sweet?

FOX You shouldn't drink, woman.

CRYSTAL And then you began to skip the places that were good in the past. And when we could have done four nights, you left after two. And then you poisoned Pedro's dog——

FOX You don't know what you're saying!

CRYSTAL You did, my love. I know you did. And I never understood why you did those things. I wondered, of course, 'cos I know you loved him. But I never understood. And maybe I didn't want to know, my Fox, because I was afraid—it was the only fear I had—I was terrified that you were

69

going to shake me off too. And I really didn't
give a damn about any of them, God forgive
me, not even Pedro, not as long as you didn't
turn on me. That's all I cared about. And now
we're back at the start, my love; just as we
began together. Fox and Crystal. To hell with
everything else.

[*This revelation stuns* FOX. *He stares at her in utter
amazement and incredulity.*]

FOX And Pedro?

CRYSTAL Crystal saw it all.

FOX You knew?

CRYSTAL I told you—I'm rotten.

FOX That I had killed the one good thing he had?

CRYSTAL God forgive me, Fox.

FOX Our friend, Pedro?

CRYSTAL What are you looking at me like that for? It
was you that did it, remember; not me. Here,
my love, sit down here beside me.

[*As if he were in a dream he goes to her and sits
beside her. She catches his hand.*]

I'd marry you a dozen—a hundred times again.

FOX Would you?

CRYSTAL Every day. Every hour.

[*She closes her eyes and rests her head on his
shoulders.*]

My sweet Fox. . . . This is all I want.

[*When* FOX *speaks his voice is very soft, almost
comforting.* CRYSTAL'S *replies are sun-drowsy.*]

FOX My pet . . .

CRYSTAL Mm?

FOX You love me, Crystal?

CRYSTAL Mm.

FOX You love me, don't you?

CRYSTAL Sweet Fox.

FOX A lot—a great lot?

CRYSTAL Mm.

FOX [*more slowly*] If you were asked to, would you go to hell with me?

CRYSTAL There and back, my love.

[*Pause.*]

FOX Crystal.

CRYSTAL Can't keep awake.

FOX I have something to tell you.

CRYSTAL Tell me.

FOX About Gabriel.

CRYSTAL He was always such a gentle boy.

FOX You don't know how they found him.

CRYSTAL Who, my pet?

FOX How the police found him.

CRYSTAL What d'you mean, my Fox?

FOX Do you remember that night he came—just after Cid and Tanya had gone—remember that night?

CRYSTAL Yes.

FOX Well, he told me the whole story that night— about what happened, and how he hid in Glasgow and then slipped over on the boat.

CRYSTAL I know.

FOX And then he told me about the reward.

CRYSTAL The what?

FOX The English police offered a reward of £100 for him: or £50 for any information about him.

[CRYSTAL *sits up.*]

I did nothing for a while, couldn't make up my mind. And then one day when we were passing through Ballymore, I went into the police station there, the white building at the end of the town, and the motorcycle policeman—remember him?

—he was there, and I—I—I told him that Gabriel
was travelling with us.

[CRYSTAL *rises*.]

CRYSTAL You?

FOX So they asked me a few questions. And then they
made me wait until they phoned Dublin. And
Dublin phoned Manchester. And that was it.
That's how he was caught.

CRYSTAL Fox . . . ?

FOX So whenever we get to Dublin next, there's £100
waiting there for us.

CRYSTAL You're lying——

FOX I don't think Gabriel knows; they probably
didn't tell him.

CRYSTAL You're lying, Fox!—you're lying!—lying!
[*She leaps at him, catches his shirt and puts her face
into his.*]
Jesus, man, deny it!

FOX It's the truth.

CRYSTAL It's a lie! Not your own son! Not Gabriel!

FOX We need the money. It'll start us off again.
[*She lets him go. She stares at him.*]

CRYSTAL Your own son? . . . To the police? . . .

FOX It's a lot of money.
[CRYSTAL *steps back from him*.]

CRYSTAL What . . . are . . . you?
[*He puts out a hand to touch her.*
She recoils. She screams.]
Don't—don't—don't touch me!
[*She backs away from him.*]
Get away from me! Don't come near me! Don't
touch me! Don't speak to me! Don't even look
at me! Must get away from you—evil . . . a
bad man. . . . It's too much . . . I don't know you.

... Don't know you at all. ... Never knew ...
never ...
[*Now she breaks away from him in a frenzy. She
lifts her coat and a case and all the time she is sobbing
and mumbling incoherently. We hear 'Gabriel ...
Never—never ... Pedro ... My boy ... Evil ...'.*]

FOX I needn't have told you. You need never have
known.
[*She has her belongings. She hesitates and looks at
him with total bewilderment.*]

CRYSTAL I don't know who you are.
[*She runs off.*
FOX *takes a few steps after her.*]

FOX Crystal!
Crystal!
[*Quietly, tensely*] It's a lie, Crystal, all a lie, my
love, I made it all up, never entered my head
until a few minutes ago and then I tried to stop
myself but I couldn't, it was poor Papa that told
the police and he didn't know what he was
saying, I don't know why I said it, I said it just
to—to—to——
[*Roars*] Crystal!
[*Again quiet, rapid*] Lies, lies, yes I wanted rid of
the Fritters and Billy Hercules, yes I wanted rid
of Cid and Tanya, and I wanted rid of the whole
show, everything, even good Pedro, because
that's what I saw, that's the glimpse I got for the
moment the fog lifted, that's what I remember,
that's what I think I remember, just you and me
as we were, but we were young then, and even
though our clothes were wet and even though the
sun was only rising, there were hopes—there were
warm hopes; and love alone isn't enough now,

73

my Crystal, it's not, my love, not enough at all,
not nearly enough.
[*Viciously turns the rickety wheel.*]
Red-yellow-black or blue, whatever it is that
tickles your fancy, now's your chance to turn a
bad penny into a decent pound, I love you, my
Crystal, and you are the best part of me, and I
don't know where I'm going or what will become
of me, I might have stumbled on as I did once,
but I got an inkling, my Crystal, and I had to
hold on to that; Crystal, my Crystal, where am I
now, my Crystal?
[*Turns the rickety wheel listlessly and sings lamely:*]
A-hunting you will go
A-hunting you will go
You'll catch no fox and put him in a box
A-hunting you will go.
[*Fairground voice*] Red-yellow-black or blue,
whatever it is that tickles your fancy, the Fox
knows all the answers—what it's all about, that's
why he's dressed in velvets and drives about in a
swank car, you're looking straight at the man that
sleeps content at night because he's learned the
secrets of the universe, strike me dead if I'm
telling a lie and you wipe that grin off your jaw,
lady, when you're at a wake, red-yellow-black
or blue, you pays your money and you takes
your choice, not that it makes a damn bit of
difference because the whole thing's fixed, my
love, fixed-fixed-fixed; [*almost gently*] but who
am I to cloud your bright eyes or kill your
belief that love is all. A penny a time and you
think you'll be happy for life.
[*A car passes. He does not hear it. He closes his eyes,*

74

puts his arm over the rickety wheel, and quickly
buries his face in his arm.]

CURTAIN

THE END